COUNTRIES OF THE WORLD

Nǐ Hǎo,
CHINA

by Leah Kaminski

CHERRY LAKE PUBLISHING • ANN ARBOR, MICHIGAN

Published in the United States of America by Cherry Lake Publishing
Ann Arbor, Michigan
www.cherrylakepublishing.com

Reading Adviser: Marla Conn MS, Ed., Literacy specialist, Read-Ability, Inc.

Book Design: Book Buddy Media

Photo Credits: ©yorkfoto/Getty Images, cover (top); ©jplenio/Pixabay, cover (bottom); ©iStock/Getty Images, 1; ©Oleksii Liskonih/Getty Images, 3; ©sofiaworld/Getty Images, 4; ©PeterHermesFurian/Getty Images, 6; ©View Stock/Getty Images, 7; ©Virginie Blanquart/Getty Images, 8; ©WanRu Chen/Getty Images, 9; ©chinaface/Getty Images, 10; ©d3sign/Getty Images, 11; ©PhotoTalk/Getty Images, 12; ©Kevin Phillips/Getty Images, 13; ©RichLegg/Getty Images, 14; ©Shannon Fagan/Getty Images, 15; ©Richard Sharrocks/Getty Images, 16; ©Lintao Zhang/Pool/Getty Images, 18; ©Muneyoshi Someya/Pool/Getty Images, 19; ©blingfashioncoltd/Pixabay, 20; ©AdrienC/Getty Images, 21; ©pidjoe/Getty Images, 22; ©sinopics/Getty Images, 23 (bottom); ©Alan Grainger/Getty Images, 23 (top); ©jameslee999/Getty Images, 24; ©salinger/Pixabay, 25; ©MoMo Productions/Getty Images, 26; ©jameslee999/Getty Images, 27; ©Studio Paggy/Getty Images, 28 (bottom left); ©View Stock/Getty Images, 28 (top left); ©Apexphotos/Getty Images, 28 (bottom right); ©Nikolai Barchan/Getty Images, 28 (top right); ©Doug Armand/Getty Images, 29 (back); ©OpenClipart-Vectors/Pixabay, 29 (front); ©P_Wei/Getty Images, 30; ©kiszon pascal/Getty Images, 31; ©kiszon pascal/Getty Images, 32; ©Frans Jo - Imageenation/Getty Images, 33; ©China Photos/Getty Images, 34; ©Phil Walter/Getty Images, 35; ©YuenWu/Getty Images, 36; ©twomeows/Getty Images, 37; ©Eugene Mymrin/Getty Images, 38; ©Xinzheng/Getty Images, 39 (top); ©Ivan/Getty Images, 39 (bottom); ©Paul Zhang/Getty Images, 40; ©Natasha Breen/Getty Images, 41; ©ansonmiao/Getty Images, 42; ©Studio Paggy/Getty Images, 43; ©Fuse/Getty Images, 44; ©Philippe LEJEANVRE/Getty Images, 45 (bottom); ©anuchit kamsongmueang/Getty Images, 45 (top); ©filo/Getty Images, background

Library of Congress Cataloging-in-Publication Data has been filed and is available at catalog.loc.gov

Cherry Lake Publishing would like to acknowledge the work of The Partnership for 21st Century Learning. Please visit www.p21.org for more information.

Printed in the United States of America
Corporate Graphics

TABLE OF CONTENTS

CHAPTER 1

WELCOME TO CHINA!

The People's Republic of China is the world's third-largest country and has the world's largest population. China's population is 1.42 billion. One fifth of humanity lives there! China is divided into 23 provinces, with several other regions, including Tibet and the major port city of Hong Kong. There are 56 different ethnic groups in China. The Han people represent more than 90 percent. Other groups are Tibetan, Mongol, and Manchu.

The Great Wall stretches 5,500 miles (8,850 kilometers) across China.

There are more than 4,000 years of recorded Chinese history. The country holds many major world sites. The Great Wall of China, the Sichuan Giant Panda Sanctuaries, and ancient cities and tombs are just some of these wonders. There are also modern wonders, such as the huge skyscrapers of Shanghai.

ACTIVITY

Practice your skills as a mapmaker. Look at the map of china above. Place a piece of paper over the map and trace the outline of the country. See where Beijing is? Mark that city with a star on your tracing. Also label the Great Wall and Tibet. Now, label the Yangtze River and the Yellow River. Do you see how the Yangtze River cuts through the center of China? As you work, pay attention to which countries border China.

China lies south of Mongolia and Russia. The country extends for 33.7 million square miles (87.3 million square km). It holds everything from massive mountains to coastal plains, and is home to the highest and one of the lowest places on Earth. Because China is so huge and varied in topography and climate, there is also a wide variety of wildlife.

Many tourists to the city of Lijiang visit its nearby mountains.

Eastern China is known for its rich farmland. Parts of the Yellow River (or Huang He) and Yangtze River flow through the region. They help bring water to the fields and rice crops. The Yangtze is the third-longest river in the world.

Many rivers flow through Hong Kong to reach the South China Sea.

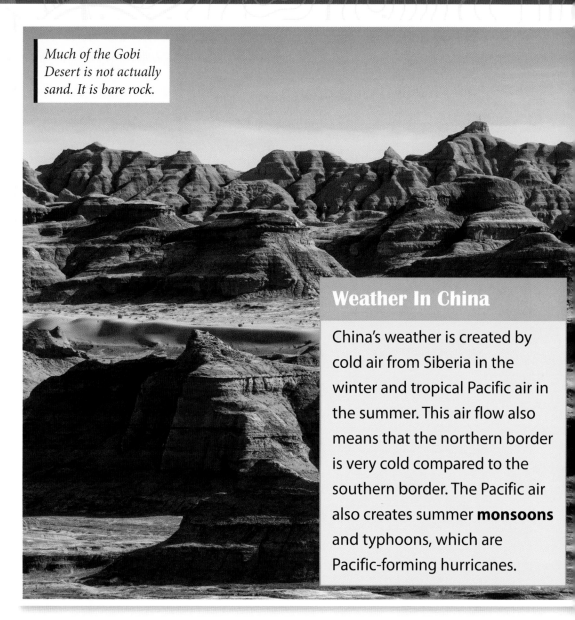

Much of the Gobi Desert is not actually sand. It is bare rock.

Weather In China

China's weather is created by cold air from Siberia in the winter and tropical Pacific air in the summer. This air flow also means that the northern border is very cold compared to the southern border. The Pacific air also creates summer **monsoons** and typhoons, which are Pacific-forming hurricanes.

In the northeast is what was once called Manchuria, a plateau with meadows, forests, and huge farming plains. Northern China is the site of the Gobi Desert, one of the world's largest deserts. Northwestern China is also home to Ayding Lake, a dry lake bed 508 feet (155 meters) below sea level. This is one of the lowest places in the world.

Southwestern China is mountainous. It includes the massive Tibetan Plateau. Part of the plateau is so high it's called the "Roof of the World." The famous mountain range to the plateau's south is the Himalayas. The Himalayas' Mount Everest is the highest peak on Earth. It is 29,035 feet (8,850 m) tall.

Mount Everest has been called "Goddess Mother of the World" and "Peak of Heaven" by native peoples.

China has many environmental problems. Air pollution is the main issue. The smog comes from cars and coal. China accounts for 50 percent of the world's coal use. A "war against pollution" is beginning to stop coal **emissions** from factories. Cities are not allowing as many cars on the road.

China's growing population and its many farms and factories have created water shortages. China already had less water than its people needed, but now about 65 percent of its water is used for agriculture and 20 percent for coal. Two-thirds of China's cities have water shortages. Factories pollute the water too. In 2014, 60 percent of major cities had bad water, and a quarter of China's rivers are dangerous to touch.

The Struggle with Smog

Air pollution in some places is so bad that people must wear masks to protect their lungs. The smog has even lowered life expectancy in some areas. In January 2013, Beijing had an "airpocalypse," during which the air was filled with 40 times the safe level of dangerous particles.

Bad farming practices, **overgrazing**, and climate change have turned more than 1 million square miles (2.6 sq km) of China into desert. The Chinese people are unhappy that the government is not doing enough to solve these problems.

A Gentle Giant

Giant pandas live deep in the mountains of China. China is their only native country. But pandas have been given to zoos throughout the world. These animals feed on bamboo. Fewer than 2,000 giant pandas still live in the wild.

CHAPTER 2

BUSINESS AND GOVERNMENT IN CHINA

China is the world's largest manufacturer. It is also the world's fastest-growing consumer market. It is the world's largest exporter and is the second-largest importer. China's gross domestic product (GDP) is currently estimated at $12.2 trillion. GDP is a way of measuring the size of a country's economy. This is the second-largest GDP in the world, behind the United States.

Millions of container ships come and go from China each year.

Around 27 percent of the country's workforce work in agriculture. Forty-five percent work in service jobs. This means they sell their time and ideas. Some key services in China are retail and financial services. Manufacturing provides 28 percent of jobs. Factory life is not easy. Workers make very little money and workplaces are often not safe.

In China, street market sales are done by bargaining. If they don't speak the same language, shop owners and shoppers often pass a calculator back and forth!

In 2016, China exported $2.27 trillion worth of goods and imported less than $2 trillion. This means it has a huge **trade surplus**. Its biggest imports are circuits, oil, iron and gold ore, vehicles, and coal. Its biggest exports are computers, broadcasting equipment, and clothes. It is the largest producer of rice in the world. China also exports electronic equipment and toys. Many of the electronic devices you use were manufactured in China.

China has stayed at the forefront of technological advances, producing cutting-edge devices and parts.

The large star on China's flag used to symbolize the Communist Party. Now the large star represents China, and the small stars represent the country's ethnic diversity.

The government of China is led by the Communist Party. Communism is a system of government that spread worldwide in the 20th century. Not many countries still follow it. The main idea behind communism is that property should be shared between all people. In practice, it is more complicated.

China was ruled by emperors for 2,000 years. It became a republic in 1911 and a communist state in 1949. In the 1970s, China began allowing some private business and ownership. Many large-scale industries, such as finance and oil, are still under government control.

Do you want to know more about China's economy? One important piece of information is its trading partners. Trading partners are the countries that import goods from a country or export goods to that country. Here is a graph showing China's top import and export trading partners.

EXPORTS

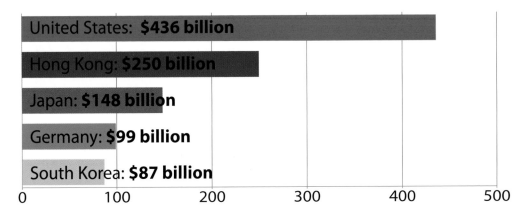

United States:	**$436 billion**
Hong Kong:	**$250 billion**
Japan:	**$148 billion**
Germany:	**$99 billion**
South Korea:	**$87 billion**

0   100   200   300   400   500

IMPORTS

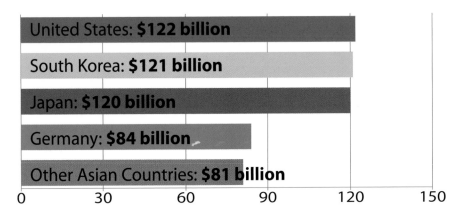

United States:	**$122 billion**
South Korea:	**$121 billion**
Japan:	**$120 billion**
Germany:	**$84 billion**
Other Asian Countries:	**$81 billion**

0   30   60   90   120   150

Delegates from across the country gather at the Great Hall of the People in Beijing for government meetings.

China's government is very complex. This is partly because the Chinese Communist Party (CCP) unofficially controls it. Under China's 1982 constitution, the most powerful government body is the National People's Congress (NPC). This is China's **parliament**, and it has nearly 3,000 members. Chinese citizens vote for these members, but the members of parliament are sometimes more loyal to the Communist Party than to their voters. This means that the CCP and executive branch are truly in control.

A Recent Political Shift

In March 2018, the Chinese constitution was changed and there are no longer term limits for the presidency. President Xi Jinping probably intends to rule for a long time. Jinping is known for worsening **censorship** and other human rights problems. For example, the government has begun collecting personal information, including DNA, to better police Chinese citizens.

Xi Jinping led a successful anti-corruption campaign that removed thousands of corrupt officials from the government in 2017.

The premier and president of China are always members of CCP leadership. The CCP selects them. The president is supposed to be a **ceremonial** position. However, the president is usually also the head of the CCP and the head of the military. This means that the presidency is actually the most powerful position in the government.

The Chinese government may be very different than those you are used to. Besides controlling industries, the Chinese government also has more control over citizens' lives. They practice censorship. This is not part of the theory of communism. The CCP believes that these methods help their country succeed.

What Once Was Forbidden...

The Forbidden City is a 178-acre (72-hectare) palace complex in Beijing. It was built starting in 1406. Access was forbidden to most people, and only the emperor could go everywhere. It is now a museum. The city was arranged to be intimidating. Its main buildings face south to honor the sun.

ACTIVITY

Research a part of China's rich history. A dynasty is a series of rulers from the same family. China's major historical eras are named for the family or clan that ruled during that time. Here's how you can learn about them.

1. There were 12 dynasties, followed by the Republic of China and the People's Republic of China. Find a list of the dynasties. Choose one to research.

2. Good researchers help narrow down their search with questions. Try making a list. Some questions you might ask are: How long did the dynasty last? Was it peaceful, or filled with conflict? What were its important technological advances? What kind of art was popular? You could ask anything you're interested in, though.

3. The next step in good research is choosing where to find answers. Ask a librarian to help you find information on your dynasty in a book or online.

Amazing Inventions

Chinese inventions have changed the world. The "Four Great Inventions" came from China. These are papermaking, the compass, the printing press, and gunpowder. China is the source of many other inventions, from as early as 7,000 BCE. Some of these are paper currency, toothbrushes, fireworks, bells, sunglasses, toilet paper, and umbrellas.

CHAPTER 3

MEET THE PEOPLE

The religions of Buddhism, Daoism, and Confucianism have been practiced in China for hundreds of years. Together they were considered the *sanjiao* ("three teachings") because people often followed a combination of them. They do not contradict each other. Each of them deals with a different aspect of life.

China has many rural villages. Many schools have only a handful of students.

Beautiful temples can be found in remote parts of China.

Confucianism, founded by Confucius, focuses on the social world and ethics. Modesty and humility are necessary in Confucianism. These qualities are part of the respectful way guests and hosts treat each other in Confucianism. Daoism was invented by Lao-Tzu. In it, nature is respected and powerful. Daoists believe we should follow nature instead of leading it. Buddhism is based on the teachings of Siddhartha Gautama of India, known as the Buddha. Buddhism teaches followers to contemplate the nature of existence, suffering, death, and rebirth.

Because China's communist government is officially **atheist**, half of Chinese people are officially atheists. China's culture is still influenced by the three teachings. Overall, the Chinese value community over the individual, which is different from Western culture. It is also part of why Communism took hold.

Confucius lived from 551 BCE to 479 BCE.

In China, many ethnic minorities wear traditional clothing. The Yao people wear hand-woven robes, jackets, and skirts.

The official language of China is Mandarin Chinese. Around 70 percent of Chinese people can speak it. There are hundreds of other local languages spoken in China.

Chinese writing is the oldest still-used system of writing in the world. It uses characters to express ideas or words. There are tens of thousands of characters. To be **literate**, one must know more than 3,000. Ninety-five percent of Chinese people are literate.

China has more than 2,500 colleges and universities. To be admitted, students have to pass a national test. Competition to get into the best schools is fierce.

In China, students spend three years in middle school and three years in high school.

In many areas of China, families share the home with grandparents, aunts, and uncles. For many years—as in many parts of the world—women were expected to obey men. This is slowly changing. Many women now work outside the home.

It is common to see three, or even four, generations under one roof in China.

ACTIVITY

Let's learn some Mandarin Chinese words and phrases. Look at the list below. On a separate sheet of paper, try to match the Mandarin words with the English translations. See the answers below.

MANDARIN

1. *qǐng (cheeng)*
2. *xiè xiè (she-eh she-eh)*
3. *nǐ hǎo (nee how)*
4. *zài-jiàn (zigh-jee-in)*

ENGLISH

a. *hello*
b. *please*
c. *good-bye*
d. *thank you*

Answers: 1-b; 2-d; 3-a; 4-c

Chinese people have a strong appreciation for art. Calligraphy, poetry, and painting are known as the "Three Perfections" in China. Statues and vessels of jade and porcelain are classic too. Jade is a type of hard, green stone. Many works of art were destroyed in the Cultural Revolution. Making traditional arts and crafts was not allowed. Since the 1980s, the government has worked to renew these artistic practices.

jade sculpture

metalwork

traditional paper craft

Buddhist carvings

A Daoist Symbol

Yin and yang is a Daoist concept central to Chinese culture. Yin and yang represent different forces that exist together in harmony, not contradiction. Yin is seen to represent a force that is cool and calm. Yang represents a force that is hot and active. Daoism says we should value both.

In Chinese art, the lotus flower can symbolize perfection, purity, long life, and honor.

CHAPTER 4

CELEBRATIONS

Houses and apartments are small in Chinese cities, so families interact outdoors and in public spaces. They visit parks, public squares, and malls. They even play billiards outside! Restaurants are also popular places for family gatherings.

Physical exercise is central to Chinese culture. People gather outside in the mornings to practice tai chi, a graceful, slow form of martial arts. They also come together to practice dance and other martial arts, such as kung fu.

Recently, video gaming and **esports** have become extremely popular. Invictus Gaming, a Chinese team, won the 2018 League of Legends World Championship. A massive esports stadium, or "town," in Hangzhou opened in 2018. The growth in esports is largely paid for by the government.

China also celebrates several national holidays, many of which have ancient roots. The people of China do not have many holidays in common with Western cultures.

Lanterns are hung during important festivals to attract a happy life and successful business.

Festival dragons are made of ornamental cloth, which covers bamboo hoops that are held up by dancers.

CHART OF HOLIDAYS

Here are some of China's major holidays. China's traditional festivals are celebrated on different days every year. This is because they use a different calendar than the Gregorian calendar of the United States and other Western cultures. The Chinese calendar is called the lunar calendar.

January or February (January 1 on the lunar calendar): **Chinese New Year**

February or March (January 15 on the lunar calendar): **Lantern Festival**

March 8: **International Women's Day**

May 1: **Labor Day**

May or June (May 5 on the lunar calendar): **Dragon Boat Festival**

June 1: **International Children's Day**

September or October (August 15 on the lunar calendar): **Mid-Autumn Festival**

October 1: **National Day and Golden Week**

ACTIVITY

Would you like to decorate your room for Chinese New Year? Try making paper lanterns. These are often a part of Chinese New Year celebrations. Here's how to make one. Try making several and stringing them together. A word of caution: these lanterns are only meant for decoration. Do not place a candle, light bulb, or other heat source inside them!

MATERIALS:

- construction paper (several colors)
- scissors
- tape, glue, or a stapler

INSTRUCTIONS:

1. Fold a piece of construction paper in half lengthwise. You should now have a rectangle.

2. Make at least 12 cuts along the fold. Space the cuts evenly. Make sure you don't cut all the way to the opposite edge of the paper.

3. Unfold the paper. Join the shorter sides of the paper together to create a tube. Tape, glue, or staple the points where the paper meets along the top and bottom of the tube.

4. For a handle, cut a strip of paper. It should be 6 inches (15.2 centimeters) long and 0.5 Inches (1.3 cm) wide. Bend the strip into an arch. Tape, glue, or staple the ends of the strip to the top of your lantern.

5. Have fun experimenting with different colors of paper.

Modern paper lanterns have a light bulb instead of the traditional candle.

Sky lanterns are made of paper with a metal frame that holds a small candle. They float much like tiny hot-air balloons.

The Lunar New Year, also called the Spring Festival, is held in January or February. It lasts for a full week, and many businesses close for parties, parades, and fireworks. Ancestors and deities are honored with the color red. This color is associated with wealth and joy. People dress in red dragon costumes and people hand out money in red envelopes.

China's Lantern Festival is more than 2,000 years old. People visit temples to pray for prosperity and light paper lanterns to honor deities. Parades last late into the night.

The city of Xi'an in northwestern China is known for extravagant New Year decorations.

China at the Olympics

China is one of the strongest countries at the Olympics. Table tennis, diving, weightlifting, and gymnastics are some of the country's best events. China didn't compete in the Olympics from 1952 to 1980. Beijing hosted the Olympics in 2008 and will again in 2022.

For the Dragon Boat Festival, there are river parades and dragon boat races. This ancient holiday celebrates loyalty and honor for the elderly. The Mid-Autumn Festival is a harvest festival that worships the moon. It is a mostly outdoor event with moongazing and family picnics. The Chinese share moon cakes for this festival. Moon cakes are sweet pies with a whole egg yolk inside.

On a dragon boat, large drums are beaten to keep the pace for rowers. A single boat might have 60 rowers!

National Day kicks off Golden Week, China's longest break besides the New Year. National Day celebrates the founding of the People's Republic of China on October 1, 1949. Golden Week is a holiday focused on shopping and tourism.

Many types of Mid-Autumn Festival moon cakes are made with intricate designs.

CHAPTER 5

WHAT'S FOR DINNER?

Grains are the staple of the Chinese diet. Rice is one important grain. Noodles, made from rice or wheat, are another. Noodles were invented in China.

Chopsticks were invented in China more than 3,000 years ago. Originally used for cooking, chopsticks are now used for eating, including rice and noodle dishes.

During a nice dinner, a cold noodle salad might be served as an appetizer.

Some dishes eaten almost everywhere for lunch and dinner are stir-fried rice and noodles, scallion pancakes, and dumplings. Most Chinese dishes are made without milk, cheese, or other dairy. Some regions use very little meat. Tofu, or soy curd, was invented in China. It is a common food throughout China.

Baodu *is a traditional Beijing snack, made of fried lamb or cow stomach with a sesame and garlic sauce.*

Chinese people often eat puddings and porridges for breakfast. Another favorite breakfast is soy milk and fried dough.

Just like so many other things in China, balance is essential to their **cuisine**. Hot is balanced by cold, spicy by mild, fresh by preserved. There is also very specific dining etiquette. Presentation is artful. Chefs use fruit and vegetables as materials to carve food sculptures.

When invited to dinner in China, it is polite to try a bit of each dish.

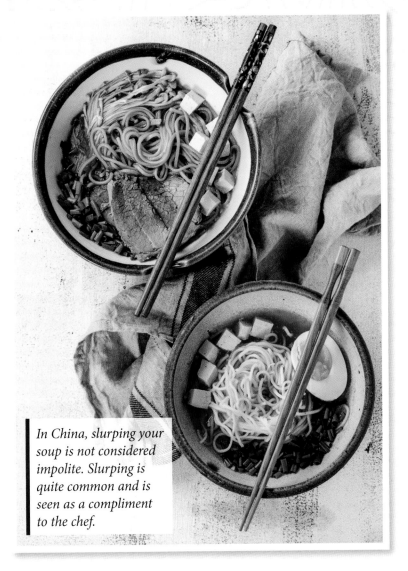

In China, slurping your soup is not considered impolite. Slurping is quite common and is seen as a compliment to the chef.

Used in many Asian countries, chopsticks were invented in China. Large, deep pans called woks are used for stir-frying, which is a kind of fast cooking that requires high heat. Soy sauce is a standard seasoning that was invented here. Other familiar seasonings are ginger, Szechuan peppercorns, sweet and sour sauce, sesame oil, rice vinegar, and chili paste.

In spite of all these commonalities, Chinese food varies greatly from province to province. Canton cuisine is eaten in Guangdong province and Hong Kong. Fresh ingredients and mild sauces are used. Seafood is popular. Roast duck and dim sum are famous dishes.

Do you like hot and spicy foods? Szechuan cuisine is right for you. Garlic, spices, and pepper are characteristic of Szechuan flavors. Szechuan dishes include cold noodles with peanut sauce and stir-fried green beans.

Wok hei *is a Chinese cooking technique. Flames from the burner are caught in the wok, giving food a slight smoky flavor.*

RECIPE

Congee is the Chinese name for rice porridge. It is very common. It is usually eaten in the mornings. It is warm and comforting and very easy to make. Make sure you get adult help when using the stove!

INGREDIENTS:

- 1 cup (185 grams) long grain white rice
- 9 cups (2 liters) water or stock (chicken or fish)
- salt (to taste)
- Optional: For breakfast, add toppings like goji berries, dried fruit, bacon, or boiled eggs. For lunch or dinner, add toppings like chopped cilantro, chopped scallions, fried garlic, or dried shrimp.

INSTRUCTIONS

- In a heavy pot, bring rice, liquid, and salt to a boil. Then turn it down so it simmers.
- Cover with a lid so some steam can still escape.
- Cook, stirring occasionally, until the rice is well cooked and the porridge is thick and creamy. This will take about 1.5 hours.
- Serve plain or with toppings.

Restaurants in China range from luxurious high-end restaurants to snack stalls on the street. There are Chinese food restaurants and foreign food restaurants of all kinds. Some restaurants offer hundreds of items, and many have pictures on their menus.

Brunch in China

Dim sum is the Chinese version of brunch. At dim sum restaurants, many different dishes are served in very small portions, along with various types of tea. Customers pick from a selection provided on a buffet or a cart taken to each table.

Many Chinese meals are served family style, where diners serve themselves from multiple dishes set on the table.

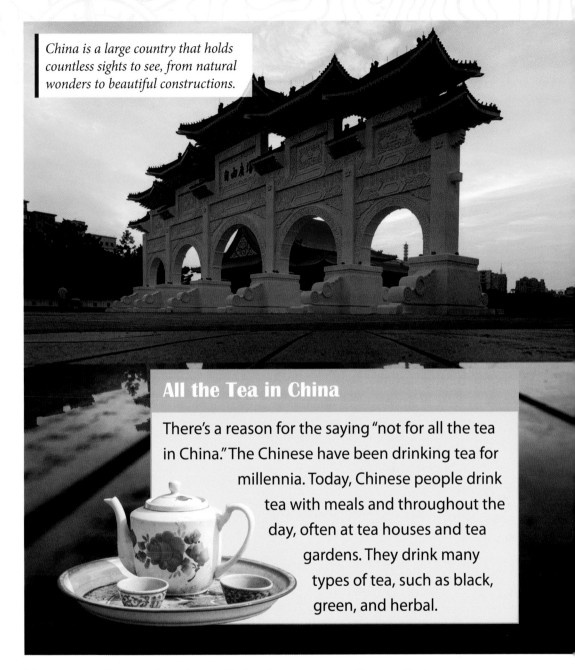

China is a large country that holds countless sights to see, from natural wonders to beautiful constructions.

All the Tea in China

There's a reason for the saying "not for all the tea in China." The Chinese have been drinking tea for millennia. Today, Chinese people drink tea with meals and throughout the day, often at tea houses and tea gardens. They drink many types of tea, such as black, green, and herbal.

Have your discoveries about China left you wanting to find out more? Your investigations don't have to stop here. Maybe one day you'll be able to visit China and soak up the wonders of this amazing country!

GLOSSARY

atheist *(AY-thee-ist)* does not believe in gods or God

censorship *(SEN-suhr-ship)* to remove or block parts of the internet, books, movies, etc. that are thought to be offensive or inappropriate

ceremonial *(ser-uh-MOH-nee-uhl)* done for show; does not have actual power

cuisine *(kwi-ZEEN)* a style or way of cooking or presenting food

emissions *(ee-MI-shuhnz)* gases and particles released into the air by engines and factories

esport *(EE-sport)* when video games are played as a competition, usually with people watching

literate *(LIH-tuh-rit)* able to read and write

monsoons *(mon-SOONS)* southwesterly winds that bring heavy rain to South and Southeast Asia

overgrazing *(oh-vur-GRAYZ-ing)* to allow farm animals to eat so much grass and plants that it causes damage to the land

parliament *(PAHR-luh-ment)* in certain types of government, the group of people responsible for creating laws

trade surplus *(TRADE SUR-pluhss)* when a country makes more money selling goods and services to other countries than it spends buying them

FOR MORE INFORMATION

BOOKS

Faust, Daniel R. *Ancient China.* New York: Gareth Stevens Publishing, 2019.

Kluemper, Michael L. and Kit-Yee Yam Nadeau. *Mandarin Chinese Characters Made Easy: Learn 1,000 Chinese Characters the Easy Way.* North Clarendon, VT: Tuttle Publishing, 2016.

Orr, Tamra. *Chinese Heritage.* Ann Arbor, MI: Cherry Lake Publishing, 2018.

WEB SITES

A China Family Adventure
https://www.china-family-adventure.com/chinese-cooking.html
Read about Chinese cooking, including common ingredients, cooking styles, and much more.

Mr. Donn's Site—Ancient China for Kids
https://china.mrdonn.org/zodiac.html
Learn more about the Chinese zodiac and find the sign from the year you were born.

National Geographic Kids—China
https://kids.nationalgeographic.com/explore/countries/china
Explore the history, geography, and wildlife of China.

INDEX

ABOUT THE AUTHOR

Leah Kaminski loves international travel. She especially likes learning about the culture and ecology of other countries. Leah lives with her husband and baby boy in Chicago, where she teaches, writes poetry, and writes books like this one.